Genre ▶ Realistic F

MW00908407

 Essential Question
How are writers inspired by animals?

Putting On an Act

by Paul Mason
illustrated by Carlos Aon

Chapter 1

At Camp

The scout leader finished assigning each den to a tent. Then he told the scouts to settle in. The boys ran down to the campsite.

Carlos and his friend Logan quickly found the Tiger den's tent. "This one's mine," Carlos said, **flinging** himself onto a cot.

Logan stared out at the forest around them. "I hope there are lots of insects here. I need to find some more so I can pass my insect study badge."

"Nature is nice to look at," said Carlos. "It's just not that interesting. You can't throw it, dribble it, or score points with it."

Logan laughed. "We're hiking the nature trail this afternoon. You might change your mind."

Carlos shrugged. "I would rather go onto the archery range," he said.

STOP AND CHECK

How does Logan feel about being in the forest?

Chapter 2

On Target

Carlos chose another arrow. He put it into place on the string. Then he raised the bow and pulled back on the string. He took aim at the **target** that he was trying to hit.

Carlos let the arrow fly. It shot through the air like a thunderbolt. It hit the middle of the yellow ring on the target.

"Not bad," Carlos thought. He almost had enough points to beat his best score.

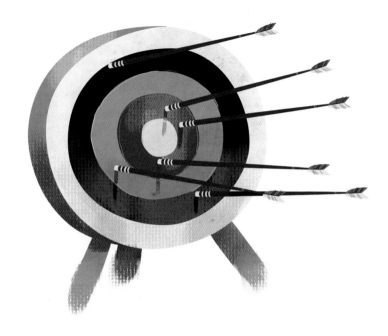

Carlos took aim once more.

"Okay, finish up," the archery instructor called. "Then we'll stop for lunch."

Carlos let loose. Again the arrow hit the target with a thud. But this time, it was buried in the black ring near the edge. That wasn't so good.

Carlos frowned. He wanted to keep practicing. He didn't want to stop for lunch. And after that, they would be going hiking.

"Why can't we do sports all day?" Carlos **grumbled** to Logan. "Why do we have to go on a hike?"

"It'll be fun," Logan said. "We might see a bear!"

Carlos still felt grumpy.

STOP AND CHECK

Why doesn't Carlos want to go on the nature hike?

Chapter 3

A Cry in the Valley

After lunch, the Tigers set off on their hike. The other boys charged ahead, but Carlos went slowly, dragging his feet.

The Tigers followed the trail until it left the woods. The trail then sloped down through a valley. Carlos slowly shuffled along, kicking his feet through the dry **brittle** twigs. The other boys got even farther ahead of him.

Suddenly Carlos heard something that made him stop. It was a cry as **shrill** as a whistle. The valley was silent for a moment. Then Carlos heard the call again.

Carlos stared at the grass along the path. At first he couldn't see what was making the sound. Then he saw something move.

A small bird was flapping around on the ground just off the trail. It was twittering loudly. One of its wings was **outstretched**. Carlos thought its wing must be broken.

Carlos watched the bird. He was fascinated. The bird was brown with a white chest and black rings around its neck.

Carlos followed the bird as it dragged itself along the ground. If he could catch it and take it back to camp, maybe they could fix its wing.

STOP AND CHECK

What happened when Carlos fell behind on the nature walk?

Chapter 4

The Killdeer

Carlos heard footsteps and shouting. The Tigers had come back to find him.

"Rule number one, Carlos," said the den leader. "Always stay with the den." Then he saw what Carlos was pointing at. "It's a killdeer," he said.

"That little thing kills deer?" asked Carlos.

The den leader smiled. "No. The name 'killdeer' is **descriptive**. It's what the bird's call usually sounds like. But right now, it's doing something quite different."

The scouts watched the bird. The killdeer called out again. It began spinning around in circles like a top. It was **fluttering** both wings quickly.

"It's hurt," said Carlos.

"No, it's not," said the den leader. "It just wants you to think it is."

"Why would it do that?" asked Carlos, surprised.

"You're the scout, you figure it out," the leader said. "Let's go, Tigers! No falling behind, Carlos."

Carlos took a last look at the little bird. He never knew birds could **pretend**. He had thought that only people could put on an act. Perhaps there was more to nature than he'd thought.

KILLDEER

Back at camp, Carlos found a book on local wildlife.

"Check this out," Carlos said, reading to Logan. "'The killdeer is famous for pretending its wing is broken. It does this to lead predators away from its young.' So that's what it was doing."

"A bird **fooled** you into following it?"

"Yes, it tricked me," said Carlos. "I must have gotten too close to its nest. It started acting like easy prey to draw me away from its babies. That's **creative**!" Carlos started making notes in his notebook.

"I can't believe you're writing about nature," Logan teased.

Carlos laughed. "I've changed my mind about nature. I'm going to work for the bird study badge!"

STOP AND CHECK

Why does Carlos change his mind about nature?

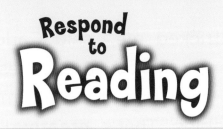

Respond to Reading

Summarize

Use details to summarize *Putting On an Act*. Your graphic organizer may help.

Details

↓

Point of View

Text Evidence

1. Who is telling this story? Use details from the text to support your answer. **POINT OF VIEW**

2. What does the word *shuffled* on page 9 mean? What clues help you to figure out the meaning? **VOCABULARY**

3. Write a description of the nature hike from Carlos's point of view. Use pronouns such as I, me, and my to show what Carlos thinks and feels. **WRITE ABOUT READING**

Compare Text

Read some haiku that have been inspired by animals.

Broken Wing

Broken wing flailing

Beckons the cat to follow.

Chicks hide behind grass.

Illustration: Rachael Tombleson

17

Rat

Sunset painted field

Footfall brushes against wheat

Sending rat scuttling.

Illustration: Rachael Tombleson

Seal

Silent ribbon drifts.

Idle seal floats on the tide,

Relishing thick eel.

Make Connections

How did animals inspire the writers of these haiku? ESSENTIAL QUESTION

What about the killdeer inspired the writers of *Putting On an Act* and *Broken Wing*? TEXT TO TEXT

Illustration: Rachael Tombleson

Focus on Genre

Poetry Poetry uses figurative language, such as similes and metaphors, to describe things. A simile is a comparison using *like* or *as*. For example, *slow as a snail* is a simile. A metaphor is a comparison without *like* or *as*. For example, *My house is a refrigerator* is a metaphor. A haiku is a short poem that has 5 syllables in the first and last lines and 7 syllables in the second line.

Read and Find Each haiku in the paired selection is inspired by an animal. In "Seal," the writer uses a metaphor to describe the eel that the seal eats. Reread this haiku. Find the metaphor. How does it help describe the animal?

Your Turn

Work with a partner. Choose a photograph or illustration of an animal that interests you. Think of some words and phrases to describe the animal. You can use figurative language. Share your words and phrases with the class.